The 7 Money Mirror
The Psychology of Financial Success

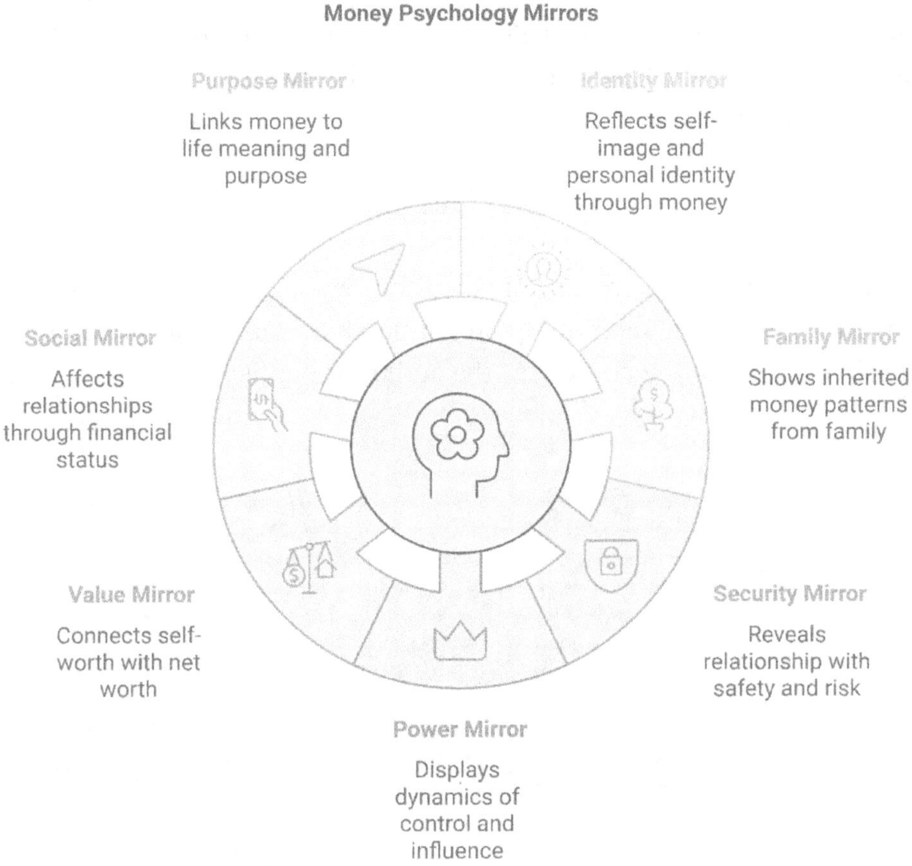

By : Ed Merid

Table of Contents

Prologue: The Money Story

At seven years old, I sat quietly on our kitchen stairs, watching my father at the table below. The moonlight cast shadows across his face as he held a crumpled bank letter in trembling hands. That night, I learned that money could make grown-ups cry. This moment became my first money mirror, a reflection that would shape my understanding of finance, emotions, and human behavior for decades to come.

Now, as a psychologist specializing in financial behavior and former Wall Street analyst, I've spent twenty-five years studying how money shapes our psyche, and more importantly, how our psyche shapes our relationship with money. I've observed billionaires trapped in self-made psychological prisons of perpetual scarcity, while individuals with modest means radiate abundance that reshapes their reality.

Money serves as more than currency; it mirrors our deepest beliefs, fears, hopes and values. Take Anna, a corporate executive earning seven figures annually. Despite her wealth, she compulsively hoards household items, her luxury apartment hiding closets stuffed with bargain toiletries. Her money mirror reflects not her success, but the echoes of her immigrant parents' struggles.

Consider Michael, who inherited substantial wealth but unconsciously sabotaged every investment opportunity, fulfilling his core belief that he didn't deserve money he hadn't earned himself. His money mirror showed his inner battles with worthiness and identity.

Our psychological makeup influences every financial decision, from daily purchases to retirement planning. Childhood experiences, cultural conditioning, emotional patterns, and core beliefs create an invisible script running continuously in our financial lives.

Research shows that emotional factors drive up to 80% of our financial decisions, yet traditional financial education focuses mainly on technical aspects, overlooking the psychological foundation of our relationship with wealth.

The seven money mirrors framework offers a path to understanding these complex dynamics. Each mirror reflects a different aspect of our financial psychology, helping us decode messages behind our money patterns and align our behavior with our values.

As a society, we face new challenges in our relationship with money. Digital technology, social media, and global connectivity create unprecedented psychological pressures and opportunities. Understanding these dynamics becomes crucial for navigating modern financial landscapes.

Through these pages, you'll learn to recognize your reflections in each money mirror. You'll understand how your early experiences, family patterns, and cultural background influence your current financial reality. Most importantly, you'll gain tools to reshape these patterns consciously.

Your relationship with money tells a story – about your past, your beliefs, and your potential. By understanding this story, you gain the power to write new chapters.

The question isn't whether your money mirrors are influencing you, they always are. The question is: are you ready to look into them with clear eyes?

Let's begin reading your reflections.

Part I: Foundations of Financial Psychology

Money, in its essence, is nothing more than a human invention; pieces of paper, metal discs, or digital numbers on a screen. Yet this creation has become one of the most powerful psychological forces shaping human behavior, relationships, and society itself. As we begin our exploration into the foundations of financial psychology, we must first acknowledge a fundamental truth: our relationship with money is rarely about money itself.

In my decades of research and clinical practice, I've observed a fascinating paradox. While we spend countless hours learning about investment strategies, budgeting techniques, and wealth-building tactics, we often overlook the psychological infrastructure that determines our financial success or failure. It's akin to trying to build a skyscraper without understanding the nature of its foundation.

Consider this: Why does a person who grows up in poverty sometimes remain trapped in scarcity thinking even after accumulating substantial wealth? How can two siblings, raised in the same household with identical financial education, develop radically different relationships with money? Why do some lottery winners lose everything within years, while others maintain and grow their windfall?

The answers lie not in financial mechanics, but in the psychological foundations that govern our money behaviors.

This first part of our journey delves deep into these foundations. We'll explore the hidden codes that shape our financial decisions – codes written by our families, cultures, and early experiences. We'll examine how these psychological imprints create the lens through which we view every financial choice, from our daily coffee purchase to our retirement planning.

Think of these foundations as the operating system of your financial life. Just as a computer's operating system determines how all other programs function, your financial psychology determines how you interact with money in all its forms. Understanding this system is crucial because no amount of financial knowledge can override a problematic psychological foundation.

What you're about to discover might challenge your existing beliefs about money. You might find yourself questioning patterns you've never noticed before. You might even feel uncomfortable as you recognize behaviors that have subtly influenced your financial life. This discomfort is not just normal, it's necessary for transformation.

As we explore these foundations, we'll move beyond traditional financial psychology to examine emerging patterns in our digital age. How does instant access to global markets affect our decision-making? What impact does social media have on our financial behavior? How are cryptocurrency and digital payments reshaping our psychological relationship with money?

Each chapter in this section builds upon the last, creating a comprehensive understanding of your financial psychology. We'll combine cutting-edge research with real-world examples, practical exercises, and transformative insights. This isn't just theoretical knowledge, it's a roadmap for understanding and reshaping your relationship with money at its most fundamental level.

Remember, these foundations weren't chosen by you, they were installed by your experiences, your culture, your family history. But understanding them gives you the power to select which elements to keep and which to transform. As we begin this exploration, maintain an open mind and a willingness to look honestly at your own money story.

The journey through these foundations will challenge you, inspire you, and ultimately empower you to create a healthier, more conscious relationship with money. Are you ready to discover what lies beneath your financial behaviors?

Let's begin our exploration of the hidden architecture that shapes your financial world.

Chapter 1: The Hidden Code of Money

Growing up in a middle-class family in Chicago, I watched my mother clip coupons every Sunday morning. She would spread newspapers across our kitchen table, methodically cutting each discount with surgical precision. At the time, I thought she was just being thrifty. Years later, as a financial psychologist, I realized she was showing me her money code – a complex set of beliefs and behaviors passed down from her own Depression-era parents.

Money codes operate silently in our daily lives, influencing choices before we're consciously aware of them. These codes form through our upbringing, cultural background, and personal history. They're like invisible scripts running in the background of our minds, shaping every financial decision we make.

Let me share Sarah's story, one of my first clients. As a successful tech executive earning $300,000 annually, she lived in a modest apartment and drove a fifteen-year-old car. Her bank account held millions, yet she felt panicked buying new shoes. Her behavior puzzled her colleagues, but I recognized the pattern. Sarah's money code was written during her childhood, watching her family lose everything in a financial crisis. Despite her current wealth, that early programming still controlled her actions.

Our money codes begin forming in childhood. Children absorb financial attitudes by observing their parents' behaviors, listening to discussions about bills, and feeling the emotional atmosphere around money decisions. These observations create lasting patterns that persist into adulthood.

Cultural influences add another dimension to our money codes. Some societies value individual wealth accumulation, while others emphasize community sharing. Religious teachings about money vary widely, from viewing prosperity as a divine blessing to considering it a spiritual obstacle. These cultural messages become embedded in our unconscious financial operating system.

The digital era has introduced new elements to our money codes. Online shopping, mobile payments, and cryptocurrency trigger different psychological responses than physical cash. Social media creates constant comparison and pressure around lifestyle and spending. These modern factors reshape our relationship with money in unprecedented ways.

Through my research and clinical practice, I've identified three core components of money codes:

1. Family Blueprints

- Inherited money beliefs
- Observed financial behaviors
- Emotional associations with money

2. Social Programming

- Cultural attitudes toward wealth
- Peer group influences
- Media messages about money

3. Personal Experiences

- Financial victories and setbacks
- Money-related relationships
- Career and income patterns

Understanding your money code requires honest self-examination. Start by asking yourself:

- What money messages did you receive growing up?
- How do you feel when making financial decisions?
- What patterns do you notice in your spending and saving?

I've seen countless clients achieve breakthroughs once they understood their money codes. Take Marcus, a talented artist who kept sabotaging his pricing because his father had taught him that "real artists don't care about money." Once he recognized this code, he could consciously choose different behaviors.

Your money code isn't your destiny – it's simply your starting point. By becoming aware of these hidden patterns, you gain the power to rewrite them. The next sections will guide you through identifying and understanding your unique financial programming.

Remember: awareness precedes change. As you continue reading, notice your reactions. They might point to important aspects of your own money code waiting to be understood.

Part II: The Seven Money Mirrors Framework

Standing in my office one afternoon, a client named Rachel held up her phone and asked, "Why do I keep checking my investment app twenty times a day, even though I know my portfolio is solid?" Her question touched on something deeper than mere financial habits; it reflected how money serves as a mirror to our inner world.

Through decades of research and clinical work, I've observed that our relationship with money reflects seven distinct aspects of our psychology. Like mirrors in a room, each one shows us a different angle of ourselves, revealing patterns that shape our financial behavior.

These seven mirrors work together, creating a complete picture of your money psychology:

1. The Identity Mirror shows how money reflects your self-image
2. The Family Mirror reflects inherited money patterns
3. The Security Mirror reveals your relationship with safety and risk
4. The Power Mirror displays control and influence dynamics
5. The Value Mirror reflects the connection between self-worth and net worth
6. The Social Mirror shows how money affects your relationships
7. The Purpose Mirror reveals the link between money and life meaning

Think of David, a successful surgeon who came to my office struggling with compulsive spending. As we examined his mirrors, we found that his Identity Mirror showed someone trying to prove

his worth through purchases. His Family Mirror reflected childhood memories of his parents fighting about money. His

Purpose Mirror revealed emptiness that no amount of spending could fill.

Each mirror offers specific insights:

- The Identity Mirror might show why you avoid looking at your bank statements.
- The Family Mirror could explain your anxiety about investments.
- The Security Mirror might reveal why you keep excess cash despite low returns.
- The Power Mirror often shows why negotiations make you uncomfortable.
- The Value Mirror frequently explains self-sabotaging financial behaviors.
- The Social Mirror reveals patterns in your money relationships.
- The Purpose Mirror shows alignment between spending and values.

These mirrors work differently for everyone. Lisa, an entrepreneur, saw in her Power Mirror a fear of success inherited from her mother. Mark, a teacher, found his Social Mirror showing why he always picked up the dinner tab, even when he couldn't afford it.

Understanding your reflections in these mirrors provides a map for change. When you know what you're seeing, you can choose how to respond. The following chapters examine each mirror in detail, offering practical tools for working with what you find.

As you read about each mirror, notice which ones resonate most strongly with you. Your reactions point to areas where awareness can lead to meaningful change in your financial life.

The goal isn't to achieve perfect reflections – it's to understand what these mirrors show us about ourselves and use that knowledge to make conscious choices about money.

Are you ready to look into your seven money mirrors?

Chapter 2: Mirror One - The Identity Mirror (How you see yourself through money)

When James walked into my office, his expensive suit couldn't hide his unease. "I make seven figures now," he said, fidgeting with his watch, "but I still feel like that poor kid from the Bronx." His words captured the essence of the Identity Mirror – the complex relationship between money and self-image.

The Identity Mirror reflects how we view ourselves through our financial lens. It shows the gap between our monetary reality and our internal self-perception. Understanding this mirror helps explain why lottery winners often return to their original financial status, or why self-made millionaires might continue working long hours despite abundant wealth.

Your Money Identity Forms Early

Growing up, I watched my grandfather, a small grocery store owner, count coins every evening. He'd say, "Money shows who you are." Years later, as a financial psychologist, I realized how this simple statement shapes many people's core identity.

Consider these common money identities:

- The Eternal Struggler
- The Natural Provider
- The Wealthy Outsider
- The Responsible Steward
- The Financial Rebel

Each identity creates its own financial behavior patterns. Take Maria, a marketing executive who grew up in a family that prized frugality. Despite earning well above average, she continued living like a college student. Her Identity Mirror showed someone who felt guilty about financial success.

Breaking the Mirror's Spell

Your money identity isn't fixed. Tom, a client who identified as "bad with money," changed his patterns by first changing his self-image. He started with small wins – tracking expenses for a week, making conscious spending choices. Each success cracked his negative money identity, allowing a new self-image to emerge.

Key aspects of the Identity Mirror include:

1. Self-Worth Connection

- How you link personal value to net worth
- Internal permission for prosperity
- Money shame or pride

2. Financial Self-Image

- Your perceived money capabilities
- Comfort with wealth
- Financial decision confidence

3. Identity Conflicts

- Professional versus personal money identity
- Cultural money values versus personal desires
- Past versus present financial self

Signs Your Identity Mirror Needs Attention:

- Feeling like an impostor despite financial success
- Sabotaging opportunities for advancement
- Persistent money shame, regardless of circumstances
- Difficulty accepting financial gifts or appreciation
- Compulsive spending to maintain an image

Practical Steps for Identity Mirror Work:

1. Notice Your Money Story

Write down phrases you use about money. Do you say, "I'm not good with numbers" or "Rich people are different from me"?

2. Challenge Your Labels

Question whether your money identity serves you. Does believing your "bad with money" help or hurt?

3. Create New Patterns

Start small. Build evidence that contradicts limiting money identities.

4. Align Actions with Aspirations

Make choices that reflect who you want to become, not just who you've been.

Real Change in Action

Sarah, a talented artist, always underpriced her work because she didn't see herself as "successful." Through Identity Mirror work, she recognized this pattern. She began pricing her art based on market value rather than her self-image. Within a year, her income doubled.

The Identity Mirror shows more than financial patterns; it reflects your relationship with success, worthiness, and possibility. By understanding your reflection, you gain the power to reshape it.

Remember: Your current money identity is learned, not innate. You can choose how you see yourself in relation to money. The reflection in your Identity Mirror can change as you do.

- What does your current financial situation say about you?
- How do you complete the sentence "People with money are...?"
- What financial identity did your family give you?
- What new money identity would serve you better?

Chapter 3: Mirror Two - The Family Mirror (Inherited Money Patterns)

"**M**oney doesn't grow on trees!" Elena heard her mother's voice in her head as she hovered over the "Buy Now" button for a new laptop she needed for work. Despite her six-figure salary, she felt the familiar grip of guilt; a direct inheritance from her immigrant parents' financial struggles.

The Family Mirror reflects our inherited money patterns, beliefs, and behaviors. These patterns run deep, often spanning multiple generations and shaping our financial decisions in ways we rarely notice.

Generational Money Scripts

Every family writes its own money story. My grandmother survived the Great Depression by hiding cash in her mattress. That fear of banks influenced my father's conservative investing style, which in turn colored my early approach to money. These inherited scripts play out daily in our financial lives.

Common Family Money Patterns:

- The Scarcity Script
- The Prosperity Gospel
- The Money Taboo
- The Provider Complex
- The Wealth Guilt

Understanding Your Family's Money DNA

Consider these questions:

- Who managed money in your childhood home?
- What financial phrases did you hear repeatedly?

- How did your family handle financial stress?
- What money secrets existed in your family?

Breaking Generational Patterns

Robert, a successful attorney, came to me puzzled by his inability to save. During our work, we traced this pattern to his father, who believed "money saved is money not enjoyed." Once Robert recognized this inherited belief, he could consciously choose different behaviors.

Key Elements of the Family Mirror:

1. Parental Money Messages

- Direct teachings about finance
- Observed money behaviors
- Emotional associations with wealth

2. Extended Family Influence

- Cultural money traditions
- Family business dynamics
- Inheritance patterns

3. Generational Impact

- Historical financial traumas
- Family success stories
- Money secrets and shame

Signs of Family Mirror Issues:

- Repeating parents' financial mistakes
- Rebelling against family money patterns
- Feeling guilty about surpassing family wealth
- Hidden money from family members
- Conflict over inherited wealth

Practical Steps for Family Mirror Work:

1. Map Your Money Heritage

Create a family financial tree showing patterns, beliefs, and behaviors across generations.

2. Identify Inherited Scripts

List money messages from your childhood. Which still guide your choices?

3. Choose Your Legacy

Decide which patterns to keep and which to change.

4. Create New Family Money Stories

Build healthy financial traditions for future generations.

Case Study: The Martinez Family

Three generations of Martinez women provided financial support to extended family members, often at their own expense. Ana, the youngest, recognized this pattern through Family Mirror work. She established clear boundaries while creating a sustainable way to help relatives through emergency funds and education support.

Healing Family Money Wounds

Financial patterns often carry emotional wounds. Jennifer avoided investing because her family lost everything in a market crash. Through understanding her Family Mirror, she developed a balanced approach to risk while honoring her family's experience.

Shifting Inherited Patterns:

- Acknowledge family money history
- Separate past patterns from present choices
- Create conscious financial boundaries
- Build new money traditions

Questions for Reflection:

- What money lessons did your family teach?
- Which family patterns serve you well?
- What financial behaviors do you want to change?
- How might your choices affect future generations?

Remember: Your family's money story influenced you, but you can write your own financial chapters. The Family Mirror shows where you came from, not where you must stay.

Chapter 4: Mirror Three - The Security Mirror (Safety and Risk Relationships)

Money and security are tightly woven together. For some, financial stability offers peace of mind, while for others; it's a source of anxiety. The Security Mirror reflects how you perceive safety and risk in your financial life. It shapes the decisions you make when balancing the need for stability with opportunities for growth.

The Foundations of Financial Security

Financial security isn't just about the numbers in your bank account. It's about your sense of safety and control over your resources. This perspective often forms in childhood. For instance, if your family struggled to make ends meet, you might equate financial security with a full pantry or a steady paycheck. Conversely, growing up in a financially stable environment may instill a sense of confidence, even during lean times.

Early experiences with money set the stage for your risk tolerance. Did your family avoid risk at all costs, sticking to safe investments? Or did they take calculated risks, viewing them as opportunities for growth? These early lessons create lasting impressions that influence how you manage your finances today.

Understanding Your Risk Profile

Everyone has a unique approach to financial risk. Some people avoid it entirely, preferring the certainty of low returns over the potential volatility of higher rewards. Others thrive on risk, drawn to the excitement and potential gains of more speculative ventures.

Your risk profile can be broken down into three main types:

1. Risk-Averse Individuals

These people prioritize safety above all. They avoid uncertainty and prefer predictable outcomes. Common behaviors include keeping money in savings accounts or low-risk bonds. While this approach minimizes losses, it can also limit growth.

2. Risk-Tolerant Individuals

This group is comfortable with uncertainty and is willing to take chances for the possibility of higher rewards. They might invest in volatile stocks, start businesses, or explore new financial opportunities. While their potential for growth is higher, they also face greater chances of significant losses.

3. Risk-Neutral Individuals

These people strike a balance between risk and reward. They evaluate each opportunity on its merits, considering both the potential gains and the likelihood of losses. Their decisions are typically guided by a combination of logic and emotional resilience.

Identifying your risk profile helps you make informed decisions aligned with your comfort level. It's not about labeling yourself as one type forever, but rather understanding where you currently stand and how your preferences may evolve.

The Emotional Side of Security

Money often carries a significant emotional weight. Fear, guilt, and even shame can surface when financial security is at stake. For some, the thought of losing money is paralyzing, while others may experience regret for not taking risks when opportunities arise.

Take David, a client who inherited a substantial sum from his grandparents. Although he had no immediate financial needs, he lived in constant fear of losing the inheritance. He kept all the money in a low-interest savings account, missing out on years of potential growth. David's fear of risk stemmed from watching his parents struggle financially; reinforcing his belief that preserving money was the only way to feel secure.

On the other hand, there's Mia, an entrepreneur who thrives on risk. She invests in startups and explores cutting-edge industries. However, her overconfidence occasionally leads to hasty decisions, resulting in significant losses. For Mia, the thrill of risk sometimes overshadows her long-term security.

Both David and Mia illustrate how the Security Mirror reflects not just financial behaviors, but also deep emotional responses to money.

Balancing Safety and Growth

Achieving financial security doesn't mean avoiding risk entirely. It's about finding the right balance between protecting your assets and allowing them to grow. This balance is unique to each individual and can change depending on life circumstances, goals, and personal growth.

Here are some practical steps to align your financial decisions with your security needs:

1. Assess Your Financial Foundation : Start by understanding your current financial position. Do you have an emergency fund? Are your debts manageable? Establishing a solid foundation reduces the anxiety of taking risks.

2. Set Clear Goals: Define what financial security means to you. Is it having enough to cover basic needs, or is it building a retirement fund that allows you to travel the world? Clear goals help you measure progress and stay focused.

3. Diversify Your Investments: Spreading your investments across different asset classes reduces the impact of market volatility. Diversification allows you to balance risk and reward, providing stability while still aiming for growth.

4. Regularly Reevaluate Your Risk Tolerance: Life events such as marriage, having children, or nearing retirement can shift your perspective on risk. Periodically reassess your financial strategy to ensure it aligns with your evolving goals.

Building Emotional Resilience

Financial security isn't just about making smart decisions; it's also about managing your emotional reactions. Developing emotional resilience helps you navigate financial challenges without succumbing to fear or impulsivity.

Here's how to build emotional resilience in your financial life:

- **Understand Your Triggers**

Identify what situations make you feel anxious or overconfident about money. Recognizing these triggers allows you to respond thoughtfully rather than react emotionally.

- **Practice Mindful Decision-Making**

Before making major financial decisions, pause and reflect. Ask yourself whether your choice is driven by fear, greed, or a genuine assessment of the situation.

- **Seek Support**

Whether it's a financial advisor, a mentor, or a trusted friend, having someone to discuss your concerns with can provide valuable perspective and reduce emotional strain.

The Role of External Factors

External factors like economic downturns, market volatility, and global events can also influence your sense of financial security. While these factors are beyond your control, you can prepare for them by staying informed and adaptable.

For example, during a recession, risk-averse individuals might feel validated in their cautious approach, while risk-tolerant investors may need to reassess their strategies. Understanding how external events influences your financial outlook helps you maintain a sense of control even in uncertain times.

Redefining Security for Long-Term Success

Ultimately, financial security is not a one-size-fits-all concept. It's deeply personal and shaped by your values, goals, and life circumstances. By examining your Security Mirror, you gain insight into how you perceive safety and risk, allowing you to make decisions that align with your unique financial journey.

Whether you lean towards caution or embrace risk, the key is to stay mindful of your choices and adaptable to change. Financial security is not about eliminating risk but managing it in a way that supports your long-term well-being.

Chapter 5: Mirror Four - The Power Mirror (Control and Influence Dynamics)

Rachel gripped her phone tightly as she checked her investment app for the tenth time that day. Despite her wealth manager's solid track record, she couldn't resist micromanaging every trade. "I need to control everything," she confessed during our session. "When I don't, I feel powerless."

The Power Mirror reflects our relationship with financial control and influence. It shows how we wield power through money, and how money sometimes wields power over us.

Understanding Power Dynamics

Money represents more than purchasing power, it embodies control, status, and influence. How we handle this power shapes our financial decisions and relationships.

Power Patterns in Finance:

- The Controller: Needs complete oversight
- The Delegator: Comfortable sharing power
- The Influencer: Uses money for social impact
- The Avoider: Shrinks from financial power
- The Power Seeker: Chases wealth for control

The Psychology of Financial Power

David, a successful entrepreneur, struggled to delegate financial decisions to his CFO. His Power Mirror reflected childhood powerlessness during his parents' divorce. Understanding this connection helped him build trust in others' financial competence.

Key Elements of the Power Mirror:

1. Control Mechanisms

- Decision-making patterns
- Delegation comfort level
- Risk management style

2. Influence Dynamics

- Money's role in relationships
- Financial boundary setting
- Wealth communication style

3. Power Balance

- Personal versus professional control
- Family money dynamics
- Financial independence level

Signs of Power Mirror Distortion:

- Excessive monitoring of finances
- Inability to delegate financial tasks
- Using money to control others
- Financial secrecy
- Compulsive spending for status

Building Healthy Power Relationships:

1. Assess Your Power Style

Examine how you exercise financial control and where it stems from. Notice patterns in your money-related decisions and relationships.

2. Balance Control and Trust

Create systems that provide necessary oversight while allowing appropriate delegation. Find your sweet spot between control and release.

3. Develop Power Intelligence

Learn to use financial power responsibly. Recognize when control serves you and when it limits growth.

Case Study: The Family Business

Mark inherited his family's business but struggled with sharing financial control. His Power Mirror work revealed how fear of losing his father's legacy drove his micromanagement. By addressing these fears, he built a more collaborative leadership style.

Practical Steps for Power Mirror Work:

1. Map Your Power History

- Track your relationship with control
- Note financial power dynamics in relationships
- Identify inherited power patterns

2. Define Healthy Boundaries

- Set clear financial limits
- Create balanced decision-making processes
- Establish appropriate oversight mechanisms

3. Practice Balanced Power

- Share financial responsibilities
- Build trust in financial partnerships
- Use money as a tool, not a weapon

The Balance of Power

Sophie, a high-earning executive, realized she used money to maintain control in her marriage. Through Power Mirror work, she developed more equitable financial practices, strengthening her relationship.

Creating Positive Power Dynamics:

- Acknowledge your need for control
- Develop trust in financial partnerships
- Build collaborative money systems
- Use influence responsibly

Questions for Reflection:

- How do you exercise financial control?
- Where might you benefit from releasing control?
- How does money influence your relationships?
- What power patterns would you like to change?

Remember: Financial power isn't about domination – it's about creating positive influence while maintaining healthy boundaries. Your Power Mirror reflects your relationship with control and offers opportunities for more balanced financial partnerships.

The path to healthy financial power involves recognizing when to hold tight and when to let go. By understanding your Power Mirror, you can build money relationships that empower rather than constrain.

Chapter 6: Mirror Five - The Value Mirror (Self-worth and Money Worth)

Jennifer stared at the work offer letter, her hands trembling. The salary was double her current income, yet she felt undeserving. "I keep thinking they'll realize I'm not worth this much," she whispered. Her words echoed a common struggle; the complex relationship between self-worth and financial worth.

The Value Mirror reflects how we measure our worth through money, and how our sense of value shapes our financial choices. This mirror shows the often-invisible connection between what we believe we deserve and what we allow ourselves to receive.

Understanding Worth Dynamics

Our perception of value extends beyond bank balances. It encompasses how we price our time, talents, and efforts. This internal value system often operates beneath conscious awareness, directing financial decisions in surprising ways.

Value Patterns:

- The Undervaluer: Chronically underprices worth
- The Overcompensator: Uses money to prove value
- The Worth Seeker: Ties self-esteem to wealth
- The Value Balancer: Maintains healthy worth perspective
- The Legacy Builder: Focuses on creating lasting value

The Psychology of Personal Worth

Marcus, a skilled consultant, consistently undercharged clients despite his expertise. His Value Mirror reflected childhood messages about money and humility. By addressing these deep-seated beliefs, he aligned his fees with his true market value.

Key Components of the Value Mirror:

1. Worth Assessment

- Personal value beliefs
- Professional worth estimation
- Social value perception

2. Value Expression

- Pricing decisions
- Salary negotiations
- Investment in self

3. Worth-Money Balance

- Income alignment
- Spending patterns
- Saving behaviors

Signs of Value Mirror Distortion:

- Chronic undercharging
- Difficulty accepting money
- Compulsive overspending
- Rejection of opportunities
- Financial self-sabotage

Building Healthy Worth Patterns:

1. Examine Your Value Story

Study the messages you received about worth and money. Notice how these beliefs affect your current financial choices.

2. Align Worth and Action

Create consistency between your skills and their monetary value. Set prices and expectations that reflect your true worth.

3. Develop Value Intelligence

Learn to separate self-worth from net worthwhile maintaining healthy financial boundaries.

Case Study: The Promotion Paradox

Sarah repeatedly declined promotions, feeling unqualified despite her track record. Through Value Mirror work, she recognized how childhood praise for humility had created an adult pattern of self-limitation.

Practical Steps for Value Mirror Work:

1. Map Your Worth History

- List messages about money and worth
- Note patterns in value decisions
- Identify inherited worth beliefs

2. Define True Value

- Assess market worth objectively
- Set appropriate financial boundaries
- Create clear value standards

3. Practice Worth Alignment

- Accept praise and payment gracefully
- Price services appropriately
- Invest in personal growth

The Worth Integration Process

Tom, a talented artist, struggled to price his work until he separated his creative worth from his financial worth. This shift allowed him to build a sustainable business while maintaining artistic integrity.

Creating Healthy Value Systems:

- Recognize internal worth
- Set fair market prices
- Accept financial abundance
- Balance giving and receiving

Questions for Reflection:

- How do you measure your worth?
- What messages shape your value beliefs?
- Where might you be undervaluing yourself?
- How can you better align worth and wealth?

Remember: Your financial worth doesn't define your personal worth, but it should reflect your true value. The Value Mirror helps bridge the gap between inner worth and outer wealth, creating alignment between who you are and what you receive.

By understanding your Value Mirror, you can build a healthier relationship with money that honors both your intrinsic worth and your financial potential. This understanding leads to more confident financial decisions and better outcomes in both personal and professional spheres.

Chapter 7: Mirror Six - The Social Mirror (Money in Relationships)

Alex shifted uncomfortably in his chair as he described his recent engagement. "I want a prenup, but I'm afraid to bring it up. What if she thinks I don't trust her?" His concern highlighted how money shapes our closest relationships, often speaking volumes when words fail.

The Social Mirror reflects how financial dynamics influence our relationships and how relationships, in turn, affect our financial decisions. This mirror shows the intricate dance between money and human connections.

Understanding Social Money Dynamics

Money flows through relationships like an invisible current, carrying messages about trust, power, and care. Whether in families, friendships, or romantic partnerships, financial interactions create lasting ripples in social bonds.

Relationship Money Patterns:

- The Provider: Defines love through financial support
- The Independent: Guards financial autonomy
- The Merger: Combines all resources
- The Separator: Maintains strict financial boundaries
- The Equalizer: Strives for financial balance

The Psychology of Financial Relationships

Lisa and James approached marriage with opposing views – she believed in joint accounts, while he preferred separate finances. Their Social Mirror work revealed how their parents' divorced influenced these preferences, helping them create a hybrid system that worked for both.

Key Elements of Social Money:

1. Trust Dynamics

- Financial transparency
- Shared decision-making
- Resource pooling

2. Communication Patterns

- Money discussions
- Financial agreements
- Conflict resolution

3. Balance of Power

- Income differences
- Spending authority
- Financial responsibility

Signs of Social Mirror Distortion:

- Financial secrecy
- Money manipulation
- Resource hoarding
- Excessive giving
- Financial dependence

Building Healthy Money Relationships:

1. Assess Your Social Money Style

Examine how you handle money in relationships. Notice patterns in financial interactions with others.

2. Create Clear Agreements

Develop explicit understandings about money matters. Address financial expectations openly.

3. Balance Independence and Integration

Find the right mix of financial autonomy and interdependence for each relationship.

Case Study: The Family Dynamic

Maria struggled with lending money to her adult children. Through Social Mirror work, she learned to set loving boundaries while supporting their financial independence.

Practical Steps for Social Money Management:

1. Map Your Relationship Patterns

- Track financial interactions
- Note emotional triggers
- Identify recurring conflicts

2. Establish Healthy Boundaries

- Set clear financial limits
- Create fair sharing systems
- Define support parameters

3. Practice Open Communication

- Regular money talks
- Respectful negotiations
- Honest financial discussions

The Integration Process

Robert and Amy faced challenges when her business success shifted their income balance. Working with their Social Mirror helped them adapt their financial partnership while maintaining mutual respect.

Creating Positive Money Relationships:

- Foster financial transparency
- Respect individual differences
- Build collaborative systems
- Maintain healthy boundaries

Questions for Reflection:

- How does money affect your relationships?
- What financial patterns do you bring to partnerships?
- Where might you need clearer money boundaries?
- How can you improve financial communication?

Navigating Social Money Challenges:

1. Family Dynamics

- Managing inheritance discussions
- Setting lending boundaries
- Addressing wealth disparities

2. Romantic Relationships

- Combining finances
- Managing debt together
- Planning shared futures

3. Friendships

- Handling group expenses
- Maintaining social boundaries
- Addressing income differences

Remember: Money in relationships isn't just about dollars and cents, it's about trust, respect, and understanding. Your Social Mirror reflects how you connect with others through financial interactions, offering opportunities to build stronger, more authentic relationships.

By understanding your Social Mirror, you can create financial relationships that support both individual growth and shared prosperity. This understanding leads to more meaningful connections and healthier financial partnerships across all areas of life.

Chapter 8: Mirror Seven - The Purpose Mirror (Money and Life Meaning)

Michael sat across from me, his recent retirement bonus untouched in his account. "I've spent thirty years chasing wealth, but now I feel empty. What's it all for?" His question echoed a universal search - the quest to align money with meaning.

The Purpose Mirror reflects how our financial choices connect to our deeper values and life mission. It shows the intersection between what we earn and what we find meaningful.

Understanding Money's Role in Purpose

Money serves as both tool and symbol in our search for meaning. How we earn, spend, and share our resources reflects our core values and shapes our life's direction.

Purpose Patterns in Finance:

- The Mission-Driven: Aligns money with values
- The Legacy Builder: Creates lasting impact
- The Balance Seeker: Weighs profit and purpose
- The Meaning Maker: Uses wealth for positive change
- The Resource Steward: Manages money responsibly

The Psychology of Financial Purpose

Sarah left her high-paying corporate job to start a social enterprise. Her Purpose Mirror showed how financial decisions reflect our deeper callings. Through careful planning, she built a sustainable business that served both profit and purpose.

Key Elements of the Purpose Mirror:

1. Value Alignment

- Career choices
- Investment decisions
- Spending priorities

2. Impact Focus

- Social contribution
- Environmental awareness
- Community involvement

3. Legacy Planning

- Generational impact
- Charitable giving
- Knowledge transfer

Signs of Purpose Mirror Distortion:

- Profit without fulfillment
- Misaligned values and actions
- Empty material success
- Purposeless accumulation
- Impact avoidance

Building Meaningful Money Practices:

1. Assess Your Purpose Pattern

Examine how your financial choices reflect your values. Notice where money and meaning align or conflict.

2. Create Purpose-Driven Strategies

Develop approaches that serve both financial goals and personal mission. Build systems that support meaningful outcomes.

3. Balance Profit and Purpose

Find ways to meet practical needs while pursuing deeper meaning through money.

Case Study: The Career Shift

David struggled with leaving his lucrative law practice to teach. Through Purpose Mirror work, he created a transition plan that honored both his financial needs and his calling to education.

Practical Steps for Purpose Integration:

1. Map Your Money Mission

- Define core values
- List meaningful goals
- Identify purpose priorities

2. Align Resources with Values

- Review spending patterns
- Adjust investment choices
- Modify career path

3. Create Impact Strategies

- Plan giving approaches
- Design legacy structures
- Build meaningful ventures

The Meaning Integration Process

Elena, a successful entrepreneur, restructured her business to incorporate environmental sustainability. This shift aligned her profit goals with her passion for planetary health.

Creating Purpose-Driven Finance:

- Connect money to mission
- Build meaningful metrics
- Design impact systems
- Plan purposeful legacies

Questions for Reflection:

- How does money serve your purpose?
- Where do finances and values conflict?
- What impact do you want your wealth to have?
- How can money support your mission?

Building Your Money Mission:

1. Personal Purpose

- Define meaningful goals
- Align career choices
- Structure spending

2. Social Impact

- Plan giving strategies
- Create change mechanisms
- Build community resources

3. Environmental Awareness

- Make sustainable choices
- Invest responsibly
- Support green initiatives

Remember: Money gains meaning through purposeful use. Your Purpose Mirror reflects how financial choices can create positive change while supporting personal growth and social good.

By understanding your Purpose Mirror, you can build a financial life that serves both practical needs and deeper meaning. This alignment creates satisfaction beyond wealth, leading to true abundance in all areas of life.

Part III: Practical Applications

After exploring the seven financial mirrors and their profound effects on our money behaviors, we now turn our attention to putting these insights into action. Theory without practice remains merely an intellectual exercise - the real power lies in applying these concepts to create meaningful change in your financial life.

Throughout my years as a financial psychologist, I've witnessed countless individuals struggle with the gap between understanding and action. Kate, a brilliant software engineer, understood her Fear Mirror patterns perfectly but felt stuck when trying to change them. James, a successful business owner, could explain his Power Mirror dynamics in detail yet found himself repeating the same controlling behaviors with money.

This section bridges that crucial gap between knowledge and application. Here, we'll roll up our sleeves and work with practical tools, exercises, and strategies that bring the Financial Mirrors framework into your daily life. You'll find specific techniques to address each mirror's challenges, real-world examples of successful implementation, and step-by-step guides for personal transformation.

What makes these applications particularly effective is their integration of both psychological insight and practical financial management. We'll explore how to:

- Convert mirror awareness into actionable steps
- Create personalized strategies for your specific patterns
- Build sustainable habits that align with your mirror insights
- Develop practical solutions for common mirror-related challenges

- Measure and track your progress

The following chapters provide concrete methods for working with your financial mirrors. Each chapter includes exercises, worksheets, and reflection prompts designed to help you implement lasting changes. You'll find case studies showing how others have successfully applied these tools, along with troubleshooting guides for common obstacles.

Whether you're dealing with deeply ingrained patterns or seeking to fine-tune your financial behaviors, these practical applications offer a structured path forward. Let's move from understanding to action, from insight to change, and from awareness to results.

The real work begins now.

Chapter 9: Breaking Pattern Cycles

We often find ourselves trapped in recurring financial habits that seem impossible to change. Whether it's overspending, avoiding budgeting, or making impulsive decisions, these patterns can feel like unshakable routines. Yet, these habits don't form overnight. They are the product of long-standing beliefs and behaviors passed down through families, shaped by societal expectations, and reinforced by our experiences.

Breaking these cycles requires more than willpower; it starts with understanding where they come from and why they persist. By identifying the root causes, you can take meaningful steps toward lasting change.

The Origins of Financial Patterns

Every financial behavior has a story behind it. For some, a habit of overspending may stem from growing up in a household where money was scarce, leading to a mindset of "spend it while you have it." For others, avoiding investments might be tied to witnessing a family member lose money in the stock market.

These early experiences shape our financial scripts—automatic responses to money-related situations. They often operate below the surface, influencing our decisions without conscious awareness. Recognizing these scripts is the first step toward change.

Recognizing Your Patterns

Start by examining your financial habits. Ask yourself:

- What recurring money behaviors do I notice?
- When did these habits begin?
- How do I feel when engaging in these behaviors?

For example, you might find that you consistently overspend on non-essentials after a stressful week. Upon reflection, you may realize this behavior stems from viewing shopping as a reward or stress reliever. By connecting the habit to its emotional trigger, you can begin to address the underlying issue rather than just the behavior itself.

Emotional Triggers and Money

Money and emotions are deeply intertwined. Anxiety, fear, and even joy can all influence how we handle finances. Identifying emotional triggers is crucial in breaking cycles.

Consider keeping a financial journal. Document not only your spending or saving habits, but also how you felt during those moments. Patterns often emerge when you track both actions and emotions.

For instance, if you notice that financial discussions with your partner consistently lead to arguments and impulsive financial decisions, this could signal an underlying fear or insecurity about money. Recognizing this can help you address the emotional root rather than continuing the harmful behavior.

Reframing Your Money Beliefs

Once you've identified your patterns and triggers, the next step is to challenge and reframe them. This involves shifting your mindset from reactive to proactive.

Let's take the example of someone who avoids budgeting because they associate it with restriction and deprivation. This belief can be reframed as viewing a budget not as a limitation, but as a tool for achieving financial freedom. By focusing on the positive outcomes, such as saving for a goal or reducing debt, budgeting becomes a means of empowerment rather than control.

Reframing isn't about denying past experiences, but about changing the narrative you attach to them. This process allows you to approach financial decisions with a mindset that aligns with your goals rather than your fears.

Building New Habits

Breaking old patterns is only part of the equation. To sustain change, it's essential to replace them with healthier habits. Research shows that consistency is key when forming new routines. Start small and build gradually.

For instance, if your goal is to reduce impulsive spending, begin by setting a simple rule: wait 24 hours before making any non-essential purchase. This pause allows you to evaluate whether the purchase aligns with your priorities. Over time, this habit can help curb impulsive behaviors and create space for more intentional decision-making.

Another effective strategy is automating positive financial behaviors. Set up automatic transfers to a savings account or automate bill payments to avoid late fees. These small steps can help reinforce new patterns with minimal effort.

Accountability and Support

Changing financial habits can feel overwhelming, but you don't have to do it alone. Sharing your goals with a trusted friend, family member, or financial coach can provide the accountability needed to stay on track.

Support systems also offer perspective. They can help you celebrate wins, no matter how small, and encourage you when progress feels slow. If possible, seek out financial communities or groups where members share similar goals. Collective learning and shared experiences often provide valuable insights and motivation.

Overcoming Setbacks

Breaking long-standing patterns is rarely a linear process. There will be moments of progress and moments of relapse. What matters is how you respond to setbacks.

Instead of viewing missteps as failures, see them as opportunities to learn. Reflect on what led to the setback and what you could do differently next time. This mindset fosters resilience and helps you stay focused on long-term progress.

For example, if you find yourself slipping back into overspending habits, revisit your financial journal or speak with your accountability partner. Understanding the circumstances and emotions that led to the lapse can provide clarity and reinforce your commitment to change.

Celebrating Progress

Change doesn't happen overnight, and it's important to acknowledge even small victories along the way. Whether it's sticking to a budget for a month or resisting an impulse purchase, these milestones are evidence of your growth.

Celebrating progress reinforces positive behavior and builds confidence. Consider setting up a reward system that aligns with your financial goals. For instance, after meeting a savings target, treat yourself to a planned, guilt-free purchase.

Looking Forward

Breaking pattern cycles is a dynamic process. As you continue to grow and learn, your financial habits will evolve. The key is to remain mindful and intentional, regularly reflecting on your progress and adjusting as needed.

By taking these steps, you can break free from limiting cycles and build a healthier, more purposeful relationship with money. This sets the foundation for achieving long-term financial success and personal fulfillment.

Chapter 10: Creating New Money Reflections

Tom stared at his bank statement, his shoulders relaxed for the first time in years. "I never thought I could feel calm looking at my finances," he said, a quiet sense of accomplishment in his voice. His journey from financial anxiety to confidence wasn't about earning more or stumbling upon a secret formula. It was about reframing his relationship with money, changing the way he thought, felt, and acted around it.

This chapter is about taking deliberate steps to build fresh financial perspectives. By reshaping your mental, emotional, and behavioral patterns, you can create a healthier and more empowering money story.

The Foundations of New Money Reflections

Changing how you see and handle money starts with understanding, three core elements:

1. **Mental Framework**: Your beliefs and attitudes toward money.

2. **Emotional Landscape**: How money makes you feel and react.

3. **Behavioral Patterns**: The habits and routines shaping your financial decisions.

Each of these elements influences the way you interact with money. Together, they form the lens through which you view your financial life.

Step 1: Assessing Your Current Reality

Before you can create new money reflections, you need a clear understanding of where you currently stand. This involves examining your financial habits, emotions, and beliefs without judgment.

- Document Present Views: Write down your thoughts about money. Do you see it as a source of freedom or stress?
- Note Emotional Patterns: Reflect on how financial situations make you feel, excited, anxious, or indifferent.
- Track Behavioral Trends: Observe how you handle money. Are you prone to impulsive spending, or do you avoid looking at your bank account?
- List Limiting Beliefs: Identify beliefs that might be holding you back, such as "I'm just not good with money" or "I'll never have enough."

Step 2: Building a Clear Vision

With a better understanding of your current financial mindset, it's time to define what you want to achieve.

- Set Specific Goals: Instead of vague aims like "saving more," decide on a concrete target, such as "saving $5,000 in 12 months."
- Establish Realistic Benchmarks: Break your goals into smaller, actionable steps.
- Define Your Desired Money Identity: How do you want to see yourself in relation to money? Confident, secure, and proactive?
- Plan Growth Stages: Recognize that change takes time. Map out short-term and long-term milestones.

Step 3: Bridging the Gap

Once you have a clear vision, the next step is to develop strategies to transition from your current financial habits to the new ones you want to adopt.

Practical Tools for Change

1. The Money Mirror Journal:

Keeping a journal can help you track your financial thoughts, emotions, and decisions. Each day, write down:

- Key money decisions you made.
- How those decisions made you feel.
- What you learned from the process.

2. The Reflection Routine:

Incorporate small, regular practices to reinforce your new habits:

- Morning Money Minutes: Spend five minutes reviewing your financial goals for the day.
- Daily Decision Reviews**: Reflect on key spending or saving decisions before bed.
- Weekly Perspective Checks: Look at your progress and adjust where needed.

3. The Growth Framework:

Use this system to develop skills and habits:

- Focus on financial literacy by reading books or attending workshops.
- Build better habits through repetition and positive reinforcement.

Case Study: Lisa's Abundance Shift

Lisa had always felt like money slipped through her fingers, despite earning a steady income. She constantly worried about not having enough, even when her finances were stable. Through structured reflection, Lisa identified her scarcity mindset—a deeply rooted belief that she must hoard money to avoid losing it all.

She began using a Money Mirror Journal to track her spending and emotions. Over time, she noticed that her anxiety eased when she allocated a specific amount for both saving and guilt-free spending. Her mindset shifted from scarcity to balance, allowing her to manage her finances more effectively and confidently plan for the future.

Step 4: Overcoming Common Challenges

Creating new money reflections isn't without obstacles. Here are some common challenges and ways to tackle them:

- **Old Thought Patterns**:
  - **Response**: Practice pattern interruption by actively challenging negative thoughts. For example, replace "I'll never get out of debt" with "I'm taking steps to improve my financial health."
- **Emotional Resistance**:
  - **Response**: Develop emotional intelligence by recognizing and managing triggers, such as stress or guilt associated with spending.
- Environmental Factors:
  - Response: Modify your environment to support your goals. If dining out is a financial drain, plan meals at home and create a more inviting dining atmosphere.
- Social Pressure:
  - Response: Set boundaries. Politely decline activities that don't align with your financial priorities and suggest alternatives.

Indicators of Progress

As you build new money reflections, you'll start noticing changes in three key areas:

1. Mental Shifts:

- Clearer decision-making.
- Reduced financial stress.
- More confidence in managing money.

2. Emotional Changes:

- Less anxiety around finances.
- Greater calm and control.
- An optimistic, balanced outlook.

3. Practical Results:

- Improved budgeting and spending habits.
- Consistent progress toward financial goals.
- Increased financial stability and security.

Step 5: Maintaining New Perspectives

New habits need reinforcement to stick. To maintain your progress, integrate the following practices into your routine:

- Regular Review: Reflect daily, weekly, and monthly on your financial habits and progress.
- Continuous Learning: Stay informed through reading, attending seminars, or joining financial communities.
- Support Systems: Build a network of accountability partners, financial advisors, or peers who share similar goals.

Integration and Daily Practices

Creating lasting financial change isn't about perfection, it's about consistency and growth. By integrating new habits into your daily life, you ensure that your financial decisions align with your goals and values.

- Start each day with a moment of reflection, focusing on your priorities.

- Make mindful financial decisions, whether big or small.
- Celebrate your wins, no matter how minor, to reinforce positive change.

Your money reflections shape your financial reality. With patience, persistence, and intentional effort, you can create a healthier and more fulfilling financial future.

Chapter 11: Digital Age Money Psychology

Alex scrolled through his phone late at night, casually adding items to his cart. The next morning, a sinking feeling washed over him as he reviewed his credit card statement: $500 gone in a matter of clicks. "It felt like I was just playing a game," he admitted, "until the bill arrived." His story is a familiar one in the digital age, where money often feels more like data than reality.

The way we interact with money has been fundamentally altered by technology. One-click purchases, mobile banking, and cryptocurrencies have redefined how we perceive, manage, and spend money. While these innovations offer convenience, they also present new psychological challenges.

The Digital Money Mindset

In the digital world, our financial behaviors are shaped by speed, accessibility, and constant connectivity. This new environment changes how we:

- **Perceive value**: Money is no longer tangible, which can distort our sense of its worth.
- **Make decisions**: The abundance of choices and instant transactions affects our ability to pause and reflect.
- **Handle impulses**: With frictionless spending, restraint frequently takes a back seat.
- **Build wealth**: New tools for investing and saving come with unique risks and opportunities.

Virtual Value and Spending Habits

In traditional transactions, money has a tangible weight: handing over cash feels different from swiping a card. In the digital space, this connection weakens. Virtual currencies, online payment systems, and contactless methods remove physical cues, making it easier to spend without immediate accountability.

Take cryptocurrencies, for example. While they offer exciting investment potential, their volatility can trigger impulsive decisions driven by fear of missing out (FOMO) or panic during market dips. Sarah, a cryptocurrency trader, learned this the hard way. Without clear boundaries, she lost significant savings by reacting emotionally to market swings. After reflecting on her patterns, she adopted a disciplined approach, setting strict rules for when and how she trades.

Digital Decision-Making: Instant vs. Informed

The digital era thrives on speed. Whether it's swiping for a ride or tapping to invest, decisions are often made in seconds. However, this speed can lead to decision fatigue, where the constant barrage of choices overwhelms our cognitive resources.

Apps and algorithms are designed to keep us engaged, often blurring the line between thoughtful decisions and automatic responses. Social media amplifies this by exposing us to curated highlights of others' financial lives, intensifying pressure to keep up.

To counteract these effects, adopting deliberate decision-making processes is essential. Simple strategies like imposing a 24-hour cooling-off period before large purchases or using budgeting apps to track spending can help regain control.

The Influence of Social Media

Social media has become a powerful force in shaping financial behavior. From influencers promoting luxury lifestyles to targeted ads offering investment tips, it creates a constant stream of spending triggers.

Comparison culture plays a significant role here. Seeing peers post about exotic vacations or high-end gadgets can spark feelings of inadequacy, leading to impulsive financial decisions. However, awareness is the first step in mitigating this impact. Curating your feed by unfollowing accounts that fuel unhealthy spending habits and focusing on content that aligns with your values can shift your perspective.

Building Digital Financial Health

Navigating the digital financial landscape requires new skills and habits. Here are key strategies to cultivate a healthier relationship with money in the digital age:

1. Awareness Tools

Use apps and tools that provide insights into your financial behavior. Track spending patterns, monitor screen time on shopping platforms, and analyze emotional triggers tied to financial decisions.

2. Control Mechanisms

Implement barriers to impulsive spending. Enable app notifications that alert you when approaching budget limits. Set up purchase delays, such as requiring manual approval for expenses above a certain threshold.

3. Balance Strategies

Establish boundaries to separate online and offline financial activities. Allocate specific times for reviewing finances and stick to them. Incorporate offline methods like writing down financial goals on paper to reinforce their importance.

Case Study: Mark's Subscription Overhaul

Mark was shocked when he realized he was paying for over ten streaming and subscription services, many of which he rarely used. By conducting a thorough review of his expenses, he canceled unnecessary subscriptions and redirected those funds toward a savings goal. This small yet impactful change highlighted the power of digital awareness and intentional spending.

Practical Applications for Digital Finance

Digital Spending Control:

- Activate spending alerts on banking apps.
- Use budgeting tools to allocate funds for different categories.
- Set limits on discretionary expenses.

Online Investment Management:

- Create a checklist before making any investment: research, risk assessment, and goal alignment.
- Avoid emotional trading by establishing clear entry and exit strategies.

Virtual Banking Safety:

- Enable two-factor authentication for added security.
- Regularly review bank statements for unauthorized transactions.
- Use strong, unique passwords for financial accounts.

Digital Wellness: Managing Tech-Life Balance

Maintaining financial health in the digital age goes beyond numbers. It requires balancing technology's benefits with mindfulness and intentionality.

Tech-Life Balance:

- Limit screen time dedicated to financial activities.
- Schedule regular tech-free periods to reflect on financial goals without digital distractions.

Financial Mindfulness:

- Before making any digital transaction, pause and ask: "Does this align with my goals?"
- Reflect on recent financial decisions to identify patterns and areas for improvement.

Digital Discipline:

- Organize apps based on their purpose, keeping non-essential ones out of immediate reach.
- Turn off non-critical notifications to reduce impulsive financial actions.

Future-Proofing Your Financial Mindset

The rapid evolution of technology means that staying adaptable is crucial. Develop habits and skills that allow you to thrive in this dynamic environment:

Adaptation Skills:

- Stay informed about emerging financial technologies and their potential impact.
- Regularly reassess your financial strategies to incorporate new tools while staying aligned with your long-term goals.

Protection Measures:

- Prioritize cybersecurity by updating software and using secure networks for financial transactions.
- Educate yourself on recognizing scams and phishing attempts.

Growth Planning:

- Invest in ongoing financial education through online courses or webinars.
- Build a diversified portfolio that reflects your risk tolerance and financial aspirations.

Finally, the digital age has revolutionized how we engage with money, bringing both opportunities and challenges. By understanding the psychological forces at play and adopting intentional strategies, you can harness the power of technology while maintaining control over your financial well-being. Each conscious click and thoughtful decision builds a stronger, more resilient financial future.

Chapter 12: Building Sustainable Wealth Mindset

David sat in his office, staring at his financial reports. "Every time I aim for quick wins, I end up worse off," he admitted. His frustration was palpable. "My father always said wealth takes time and discipline, but patience isn't my strong suit." His story isn't unique. Many of us are enticed by the allure of immediate gains, but true, lasting wealth demands a different mindset, one rooted in sustainability.

This chapter explores how to cultivate a mindset that prioritizes long-term growth, resilience, and stability. It's about shifting from reactive, short-term decisions to a deliberate, future-focused strategy.

Core Principles of a Sustainable Wealth Mindset

Building wealth sustainably requires a blend of mental clarity, emotional balance, and disciplined behavior. Let's break down the essential components:

1. Value-Based Decision-Making

Sustainable wealth begins with understanding what truly matters. Every financial decision should align with your long-term values and goals.

- Long-Term Perspective: Evaluate decisions not just for immediate returns but for their impact over months or even years.
- Strategic Planning: Set clear, achievable objectives and map out the steps to get there.
- Ethical Considerations: Build wealth in ways that align with your moral and social values.
- Resource Optimization: Maximize the efficiency of your time, money, and energy.

2. Growth-Oriented Thinking

Wealth isn't just about accumulating money, it's about evolving your skills, knowledge, and opportunities.

- Compound Growth: Understand how small, consistent actions can lead to exponential returns over time.
- Continuous Learning: Stay informed about financial trends and investment strategies.
- Skill Development: Enhance your ability to generate and manage wealth effectively.
- Opportunity Recognition: Learn to identify and seize growth opportunities.

3. Risk Intelligence

Rather than avoiding risk altogether, sustainable wealth builders learn to manage it effectively.

- Calculated Risks: Assess potential downsides and ensure you can recover if things don't go as planned.
- Portfolio Balance: Diversify investments to spread risk and stabilize returns.
- Market Understanding: Develop a solid grasp of market dynamics to make informed decisions.
- Protection Strategies: Safeguard your wealth through insurance, emergency funds, and legal measures.

The Psychological Foundation of Wealth

1. Mental Framework

Your mindset shapes your financial reality. Transitioning from a scarcity mentality to one of abundance is crucial.

- **Abundance Thinking**: Believe that wealth can grow without depriving others.

- **Growth Mindset**: View challenges as opportunities for improvement.
- **Patient Perspective**: Understand that building wealth is a marathon, not a sprint.
- **Strategic Vision**: Keep your eye on long-term goals, even when short-term gains tempt you.

2. Emotional Management

Emotions often drive financial decisions, sometimes to our detriment. Developing emotional intelligence can help you stay grounded.

- Fear Control: Don't let fear of loss paralyze you from taking calculated risks.
- Greed Regulation: Avoid the trap of chasing returns without a solid plan.
- Stress Handling: Financial ups and downs are inevitable. Learn to navigate them calmly.
- Confidence Building: Trust in your strategy and the systems you've built.

3. Behavioral Systems

Sustainable wealth requires consistent actions backed by robust systems.

- **Consistent Habits**: Develop routines like regular savings, investing, and financial reviews.
- **Disciplined Execution**: Stick to your plan even when emotions or market conditions sway you.
- **Regular Review**: Periodically assess your progress and adjust strategies as needed.
- **Adaptive Responses**: Be flexible enough to pivot when circumstances change.

Case Study: Maria's Journey to Sustainable Wealth

Maria was a marketing professional who initially approached investing with an aggressive, short-term mindset. She frequently traded stocks based on market trends, hoping for quick profits. However, after a significant loss, she realized the importance of a more disciplined approach.

Over the next five years, Maria adopted a sustainable wealth mindset. She diversified her portfolio, made regular contributions to index funds, and focused on long-term growth. By leveraging the power of compound interest, she steadily built her wealth while reducing stress and emotional decision-making.

Practical Steps to Build a Sustainable Wealth Mindset

Daily Practices

- **Financial Review**: Spend a few minutes reviewing your transactions and investments.
- **Knowledge Building**: Read articles or watch videos about personal finance and markets.
- **Mindful Spending**: Reflect on whether each purchase aligns with your goals.

Weekly Routines

- **Portfolio Check**: Ensure your investments are balanced and aligned with your risk tolerance.
- **Progress Tracking**: Compare your financial actions to your short-term goals.
- **Goal Adjustment**: Reassess priorities and make necessary changes to your plan.

Monthly Actions

- **Performance Review**: Analyze how your investments and savings are performing.
- **Resource Allocation**: Reallocate funds based on new insights or changing needs.
- **Risk Assessment**: Identify any new risks and adjust your protection strategies accordingly.

Overcoming Common Challenges

Sustainable wealth building isn't without obstacles. Here's how to navigate them:

- **Short-Term Thinking**: Use visual reminders of your long-term goals to counteract impulsive decisions.
- **Emotional Decisions**: Pause before making financial moves during emotional highs or lows.
- **Market Volatility**: Trust in your diversified strategy and avoid reactionary selling.
- **External Pressure**: Stay focused on your goals, even when others question your approach.

Key Indicators of Success

1. Financial Metrics

- Steady growth in net worth
- Consistent savings and investment returns
- Effective risk management

2. Personal Development

- Expanded financial knowledge
- Improved decision-making skills
- Stronger professional and social networks

3. Life Impact

- Reduced financial stress
- Achieving personal and family goals
- Creating a legacy for future generations

Sustaining Wealth Over Time

A sustainable wealth mindset is a lifelong endeavor. Here's how to maintain it:

Regular Assessment

- Continuously review your financial goals, strategies, and outcomes.

Continuous Growth

- Invest in your personal and professional development to stay ahead in an evolving financial landscape.

Balanced Life Integration

- Ensure your financial pursuits support, rather than detract from, your overall well-being.

To conclude, building wealth sustainably is about more than accumulating assets; it's about cultivating habits, making intentional choices, and committing to lifelong learning. With patience and persistence, you can create a financial foundation that supports not just your goals, but also your values and aspirations.

Part IV: Integration and Growth

Financial success isn't just about understanding concepts or executing strategies in isolation. It's about how these elements come together to form a cohesive system that supports lasting growth. This part of the book focuses on integrating the knowledge, habits, and mindset cultivated so far, turning them into a dynamic framework that adapts and evolves with your financial goals.

Wealth building is a continuous process, not a static achievement. As life circumstances and economic landscapes shift, so must your approach. To thrive, it's essential to strike a balance between stability and flexibility. This means refining your systems, leveraging past lessons, and staying open to new opportunities that align with your long-term vision.

Integration bridges the gap between theory and practice. It ensures that your financial decisions are not only effective in isolation but also contribute to a broader, sustainable wealth strategy. Growth, on the other hand, requires an intentional focus on expanding both your financial and personal capacities. Together, these concepts form the foundation for enduring success.

This section will guide you through strategies to harmonize your financial practices, amplify their impact, and cultivate resilience in the face of change. Whether you're refining your investment approach, optimizing your income streams, or aligning your wealth-building efforts with your life goals, this part provides a roadmap for sustainable progress.

By the end, you'll have a holistic framework that not only supports financial well-being but also enhances your overall quality of life. Let's explore how integration and growth can work hand in hand to propel you toward a more secure and fulfilling financial future.

Chapter 13: The Mirror Method - Daily Practices

Rachel sat across from me, holding her financial journal tightly. "Every time I reflect on my spending at the end of the day," she shared, "a pattern emerges. The days I'm stressed at work are the days I splurge on things I don't even need." This simple observation, made possible through a daily practice, transformed her approach to money. What was once a cycle of impulsive spending became a system of intentional financial decisions?

The "Mirror Method" is rooted in the idea that small, consistent actions reveal deep insights about your financial habits. Each day provides an opportunity to reflect on decisions through seven lenses, or mirrors, designed to align your daily practices with long-term financial growth.

The Power of Daily Practice

Financial success doesn't happen in giant leaps but in the accumulation of steady, intentional steps. The Mirror Method harnesses the routine of reflection to create actionable insights that drive smarter decisions. This practice allows you to shift from reactive financial behaviors to proactive wealth building.

Daily Mirror Practices

The day unfolds in three distinct phases, each offering opportunities to engage with your financial habits:

1. Morning Reflection

Start your day with clarity and intention.

- Set financial goals for the day: What do you want to achieve today?
- Review your spending plan: Ensure that your planned expenses align with your larger objectives.

- Prepare your mindset: Ground yourself in the values and priorities that will guide your decisions.

2. Daytime Awareness

Throughout the day, moments of choice arise. These are critical points where mindful engagement with your financial habits can prevent impulsive decisions.

- Pause before purchases: Ask yourself if this expense aligns with your daily goals.
- Document decisions: Keep a quick log of your spending and the context surrounding each purchase.
- Track emotional triggers: Recognize how feelings influence your financial behavior.

3. Evening Review

End the day by consolidating your insights.

- Analyze your transactions: Review what you spent and why.
- Spot recurring patterns: Look for habits or triggers that consistently drive your financial choices.
- Plan adjustments for tomorrow: Refine your approach based on what you learned today.

The Seven Money Mirrors in Action

Each of the seven mirrors provides a unique perspective, helping you reflect on specific aspects of your financial life:

1. Identity Mirror

Your financial choices reflect your self-perception.

- Are your income and career aligned with your sense of self-worth?
- How are you investing in your personal and professional growth?

2. Values Mirror

Your spending should reflect your core values.

- Do your purchases align with your priorities?
- Are you allocating resources toward what truly matters?

3. Family Mirror

Family influences shape many financial habits.

- Are your money behaviors rooted in learned patterns?
- How are you contributing to or redefining your family's financial legacy?

4. Security Mirror

Financial security is a cornerstone of sustainable wealth.

- Are you managing risks effectively?
- Have you implemented safeguards like emergency funds and insurance?

5. Power Mirror

Money is a tool for control and influence.

- Are you making decisions that enhance your financial autonomy?
- How do you assert control over your financial boundaries?

6. Freedom Mirror

Financial freedom means having choices.

- Are your decisions expanding or limiting your options?
- What constraints are you actively working to remove?

7. Legacy Mirror

Your wealth carries the potential for impact beyond your lifetime.

- Are you building a financial legacy that aligns with your values?
- How are you preparing to pass on wealth and wisdom to future generations?

Practical Applications of the Mirror Method

The Mirror Method becomes most effective when integrated into structured routines and systems.

1. Morning Routine

- Spend five minutes setting your financial intention.
- Review any upcoming expenses or financial commitments.
- Align your goals with the broader vision of what you're working toward.

2. Mid-Day Check-In

- Take a moment to assess your progress.
- Identify any deviations from your plan and correct course if necessary.
- Track emotional or situational triggers influencing your financial decisions.

3. Evening Process

- Dedicate time to review your day's transactions and financial behaviors.
- Record observations and insights in a financial journal.
- Make a plan for any adjustments to improve tomorrow's financial choices.

Tools and Strategies for Success

To fully integrate daily practices, consider using tools and systems that streamline the process:

- Digital Tools: Budgeting apps, financial trackers, and digital journals.
- Physical Tools: Traditional journals, reflection cards, or printed tracking sheets.
- Support Systems: Accountability partners or professional financial advisors can provide additional guidance and motivation.

Overcoming Challenges

Daily reflection isn't always easy. However, anticipating challenges can help you stay consistent.

1. Time Constraints

- Keep routines short and efficient. Use tools to streamline tracking and analysis.

2. Consistency Issues

- Start with one practice and gradually build as it becomes habitual.
- Pair reflection with existing habits, like reviewing finances with your morning coffee.

3. Emotional Resistance

- Face uncomfortable financial realities with curiosity rather than judgment.
- Celebrate small wins to maintain motivation and momentum.

Measuring Progress

Success in the Mirror Method is reflected in three main areas:

1. Behavioral Changes

- Improved decision-making and reduced impulsive spending.
- Greater alignment between financial behavior and personal values.

2. Financial Outcomes

- More consistent savings and strategic investments.
- Better risk management and security planning.

3. Personal Growth

- Increased financial literacy and confidence.
- Enhanced self-awareness and emotional regulation in money matters.

Building Momentum for Long-Term Success

The Mirror Method is a practice of steady improvement. Each day offers an opportunity to refine your habits and deepen your understanding of your financial psychology. Over time, these small steps lead to significant financial and personal growth.

By embedding daily reflection into your routine, you're not just managing money, you're cultivating a mindset for sustainable wealth.

Chapter 14: Financial Decision Framework

Tom, a successful architect, sat across from me, grappling with a critical investment decision. "The numbers make sense," he said, "but something feels off." His intuition, honed by years of professional and personal experience, flagged risks that his spreadsheets couldn't reveal. This scenario underscores a powerful truth: sound financial decisions arise from a blend of logical analysis and emotional intelligence.

The "Financial Decision Framework" bridges the gap between data and instinct. It offers a structured approach to navigate financial choices confidently, ensuring both practical and psychological alignment.

Core Components of the Framework

1. Clarity: Define the Decision

Every effective decision begins with clarity. What are you trying to achieve? Whether it's a long-term investment, a significant purchase, or debt repayment, defining your goals sets the stage for success.

- **Set Clear Objectives**: Know your desired outcome. For instance, are you aiming for asset growth, income stability, or risk reduction?
- **Understand the Context**: Consider the financial, personal, and market conditions surrounding the decision.
- **Establish Boundaries**: Identify your constraints, budget, time frame, or acceptable risk.

This clarity helps focus on decisions that align with your overall strategy, filtering out irrelevant distractions.

2. Evaluation: Analytical and Emotional Balance

Once the decision is clear, the next step involves evaluating your options. Effective decision-making requires a balance between hard data and emotional insights.

Analytical Evaluation

- **Data Gathering**: Collect relevant facts—performance histories, market trends, or financial forecasts.
- **Risk Assessment**: Identify potential pitfalls. What's the likelihood of failure, and what would the consequences be?
- **Cost-Benefit Analysis**: Weigh potential gains against the risks and costs.

Emotional Check-In

While data provides a rational basis, your emotions offer a nuanced layer of insight. Ignoring these feelings could lead to poor choices or unnecessary stress.

- **Intuition**: Pay attention to gut reactions. These often reflect subconscious pattern recognition.
- **Stress and Comfort Levels**: If a decision causes undue anxiety, it may not align with your risk tolerance.
- **Fear and Excitement**: Differentiate between productive caution and fear-driven avoidance.

By synthesizing these evaluations, you can make decisions that feel both rational and right.

3. Integration: Aligning Data and Emotion

The real power of this framework lies in integration. Here, the logical and emotional evaluations converge to form a cohesive action plan.

- **Identify Contradictions**: Pinpoint areas where your data analysis and emotional reactions diverge.
- **Resolve Conflicts**: Explore the reasons behind these conflicts. Are they based on incomplete data or personal biases?
- **Create an Action Plan**: Formulate a step-by-step approach that accounts for both logical insights and emotional considerations.

Applying the Framework in Real Life

Let's apply the framework across various financial scenarios to illustrate its versatility.

Investment Decisions

Investments often involve a high degree of uncertainty. Applying the framework can help balance potential rewards against the associated risks.

- **Clarity**: Define your investment objective—capital growth, steady income, or diversification.
- **Evaluation**: Analyze the historical performance of your options and align them with your risk tolerance. Don't ignore feelings of unease; they might signal hidden risks.
- **Integration**: Start small, allowing your data-driven confidence and emotional comfort to grow in tandem.

Major Purchases

Whether buying a home or starting a business, significant purchases require careful consideration.

- **Clarity**: What's your primary goal? Are you looking for a long-term investment or immediate utility?
- **Evaluation**: Compare options by analyzing costs, benefits, and emotional alignment. For instance, does a house that ticks every box still leave you with doubts?

- **Integration**: Ensure the purchase aligns with both financial logic and personal values.

Debt Management

Managing debt effectively is critical to financial well-being.

- Clarity: Understand the full scope of your debt, including interest rates and repayment terms.
- Evaluation: Compare repayment strategies to find the one that offers the best balance between cost and emotional peace.
- Integration: Implement a plan that prioritizes high-interest debt while maintaining your financial stability.

Decision Tools and Techniques

Integrating the Financial Decision Framework with specific tools enhances its practical utility.

Analytical Tools

- **Budgeting Software**: Provides real-time insights into income, expenses, and cash flow.
- **Investment Platforms**: Offer advanced analytics and forecasting for more informed decisions.
- **Spreadsheets**: Simplify complex calculations, especially for comparing financial scenarios.

Emotional Tools

- **Decision Journals**: Document your emotional and logical thought processes to refine future decisions.
- **Stress and Comfort Scales**: Measure your emotional state to gauge alignment with the decision.

Integration Tools

- Decision Matrices: Compare multiple options side by side.
- Action Planners: Translate decisions into actionable steps with timelines and milestones.

Avoiding Common Pitfalls

Even with a solid framework, certain pitfalls can derail the decision-making process. Recognizing and addressing them is crucial.

1. Analysis Paralysis

Endless data collection and comparison can delay decisions. To avoid this, set deadlines for each evaluation phase and focus on key metrics.

2. Emotional Override

Emotions like fear and greed can cloud judgment. Use emotional check-ins to identify when feelings may be disproportionately influencing your choices.

3. Overconfidence

Assuming you've accounted for everything can lead to blind spots. Regularly review decisions with trusted advisors or peers to gain fresh perspectives.

Measuring Success

The effectiveness of the Financial Decision Framework is evident in three key areas:

- Financial Outcomes: Improved returns, reduced debt, and optimized spending.
- Behavioral Shifts: Greater consistency in financial habits and reduced impulsive decisions.
- Personal Confidence: Enhanced peace of mind and a stronger sense of control over financial matters.

The Financial Decision Framework empowers you to make informed, balanced decisions. By harmonizing analytical rigor with emotional insight, you not only improve financial outcomes but also build a sustainable decision-making system that grows with you.

Chapter 15: Future Money Reflections

Lisa, a digital currency analyst, shared an insightful observation: "Money isn't just changing form, our entire relationship with it is shifting. The psychological impact runs deeper than most people realize."

As technology reshapes financial systems, the psychological connection we have to money evolves. This chapter will help you understand and prepare for these changes, blending personal reflection with an awareness of broader societal shifts. The future of money is not just about technological advancements, but how those advancements influence individual behaviors, decisions, and ultimately, our sense of financial well-being.

Emerging Trends in the Future of Money

The landscape of money is rapidly changing. Traditional financial systems are being supplemented, and in some cases, replaced, by new technologies, social structures, and evolving behaviors. It's crucial to stay ahead of these changes while maintaining a stable, grounded approach to your financial choices.

1. Digital Evolution

- **Cryptocurrency Impact**: Cryptocurrencies like Bitcoin and Ethereum are becoming more mainstream. They offer new ways to store value, invest, and transact, challenging traditional banking systems. However, the volatility and regulatory uncertainties also introduce new risks that require careful consideration.

- **Digital Payment Systems**: Mobile payments and digital wallets have replaced physical wallets for many people. This convenience has shifted the way we manage our day-to-day finances, making it easier to spend but also harder to track.

- **Virtual Banking Growth**: Online banking and neobanks are emerging as alternatives to traditional banks, providing financial services without the physical infrastructure.
- **Blockchain Applications**: Beyond cryptocurrency, blockchain is reshaping industries from supply chains to real estate, providing greater transparency and security in financial transactions.

2. Social Changes

- **Community-Based Finance**: Platforms like crowdfunding and peer-to-peer lending have enabled individuals to invest in community-driven projects and support each other financially, bypassing traditional institutions.
- **Social Impact Investing**: There's a growing emphasis on investments that generate positive social or environmental impacts, as consumers align their financial decisions with their personal values.
- **Collaborative Economics**: The rise of the sharing economy (think: Uber, Airbnb) is changing the way we think about ownership, value exchange, and financial involvement.

3. Behavioral Shifts

- **Digital Spending Patterns**: As digital wallets and credit card spending become the norm, people may become more detached from the value of money, leading to less mindful spending.
- **Virtual Asset Ownership**: Digital assets like NFTs (non-fungible tokens) are gaining attention. While they offer a new form of ownership, their value and longevity are still uncertain.
- **Online Trading Psychology**: The rise of online trading platforms has made stock trading more accessible but also more impulsive. Behavioral biases like fear and greed are amplified when you can trade at the touch of a button.

- **Digital Wealth Perception**: As wealth is increasingly tied to virtual and digital assets, the line between real and perceived wealth blurs, influencing how individuals make financial decisions.

Psychological Adaptations to Future Financial Realities

Understanding these trends is only part of the equation. To adapt to this new world, we must also adjust how we perceive and interact with money on a psychological level.

1. Money Perception

- **Value Understanding**: As money shifts forms, we must continually redefine what it means for something to have value. Is it the currency itself, the asset it represents, or the security it provides?
- **Asset Recognition**: In the digital age, traditional assets like property and cash are being joined by intangible assets like data and digital currency. Recognizing and valuing these assets requires a shift in mindset.
- **Worth Calculation**: With new technologies and decentralized financial systems, calculating wealth and worth may no longer follow traditional formulas. This opens up possibilities for a more nuanced approach to wealth building.
- **Risk Evaluation**: New financial tools come with new risks. Evaluating these risks; whether they're related to volatile cryptocurrencies or new types of investments; requires both analytical skills and emotional awareness.

2. Financial Behavior

- **Spending Patterns**: The ease of digital spending can encourage impulsive behavior. Without physical money, it's easy to lose track of how much is being spent. A heightened awareness of spending habits and regular reflection on these choices can help counteract this trend.

- **Saving Habits**: With the rise of digital investments and decentralized finance, saving is becoming more complex. Instead of simple bank accounts, people may consider investments in stocks, bonds, crypto, and other assets.

- **Investment Approaches**: Future financial choices require us to consider both traditional investment strategies and emerging options like cryptocurrency or socially responsible investing. Understanding and balancing these is key to long-term wealth accumulation.

- **Security Practices**: As we move into an increasingly digital world, security measures like identity protection and safeguarding online assets are paramount. Financial decisions must now include proactive steps to protect personal data and digital assets.

3. Decision-Making

- **Choice Processes**: As financial options expand, making informed, intentional decisions becomes more complex. It's crucial to have frameworks that guide your decisions, weighing both emotional and logical factors.

- **Risk Assessment**: Financial choices are rarely risk-free. Understanding your own tolerance for risk, and adjusting your decision-making process accordingly, becomes vital in an unpredictable financial environment.

- **Value Judgment**: The lines between traditional and digital assets are increasingly blurred. Evaluating what has value in this new landscape will require both strategic thinking and emotional intelligence.

- **Control Mechanisms**: As technology makes it easier to invest, save, and spend, retaining control over your financial life becomes more challenging. It's essential to create boundaries that allow you to make decisions that align with your values and long-term goals.

Technology Integration in Financial Decision-Making

Technology continues to play a major role in reshaping financial systems. However, it is not simply about incorporating new tools but understanding their impact on decision-making.

1. Digital Tools

- **AI Advisors**: Artificial intelligence is becoming a key player in personal finance, offering automated investment advice and financial planning.
- **Automated Systems**: Many financial tasks, from savings to investment, can now be automated. These systems can help you save money or invest according to preset rules, reducing emotional bias in decision-making.
- **Smart Contracts**: The rise of blockchain technology has introduced smart contracts, which automatically execute transactions based on predefined conditions, reducing the need for intermediaries.
- **Predictive Analytics**: Using data to forecast trends, predict market behavior, and make financial decisions is becoming more common, helping investors make better-informed choices.

2. Security Measures

- **Identity Protection**: As digital financial transactions become the norm, protecting your identity from theft becomes increasingly critical.

- **Asset Safeguarding**: With cryptocurrencies and online investments, securing digital wallets and other virtual assets is essential.

- **Privacy Maintenance**: Financial decisions now require consideration of how personal data is being shared, especially in a world where data is as valuable as currency.

- **Risk Management**: Understanding the risks inherent in emerging technologies, such as cybersecurity threats, and managing those risks is a new aspect of financial decision-making.

3. Interface Design

- **User Interaction**: The way financial tools are designed can influence decision-making. Clear, intuitive interfaces can help users make better choices by providing relevant information and feedback.

- **Information Display**: How information is presented matters. With complex financial data, presenting it in a digestible, actionable format helps decision-making processes.

- **Decision Support**: Tools that help you weigh the pros and cons of different financial choices, based on your unique circumstances, will be a key part of navigating the future of money.

Adapting to the Future: Strategies for Success

As these changes unfold, it's important to develop the skills, mindset, and strategies necessary to adapt.

1. Skill Development

- **Digital Literacy**: Understanding new financial technologies and platforms is critical. Keeping up with digital trends will allow you to make informed decisions in a fast-evolving financial environment.

- **Risk Awareness**: Recognizing and understanding risks associated with digital assets, cryptocurrency, and even the potential volatility of traditional markets is key to long-term success.

- **Security Practices**: Strengthening your knowledge of online security and privacy measures will safeguard both your personal information and your investments.

- **Decision-Making Skills**: Refining your ability to make clear, thoughtful decisions, even in the face of uncertainty, will empower you in the future of money.

2. Mindset Evolution

- **Flexibility Building**: As the financial landscape evolves, being adaptable will be your greatest strength. Keep an open mind and a willingness to change.

- **Change Acceptance**: Embracing new technologies and financial strategies is crucial. Those who resist change may find themselves left behind.

- **Pattern Recognition**: Being able to identify emerging patterns, whether in the markets or in your own financial behavior, will give you a significant advantage.

- **Growth Orientation**: Cultivating a mindset focused on growth and learning will help you adapt to the challenges and opportunities the future holds.

3. Balance Maintenance

- **Physical-Digital Integration**: It's important to find a balance between digital financial systems and traditional methods. Use the convenience of digital tools while ensuring you maintain control over your financial decisions.

- **Value Preservation**: As the forms of money evolve, it's essential to preserve the values that matter most to you, whether that's saving for future goals, ethical investing, or prioritizing financial security.

- **Control Retention**: Stay proactive in managing your financial choices. Even with automation and AI, retaining a sense of control over your money is vital.
- **Security Enhancement**: Regularly updating your security practices and staying informed about new threats will ensure that you continue to protect both your financial data and your wealth.

The future of money is full of new possibilities, yet it also presents challenges that require both awareness and preparation. By adapting to these changes, through developing relevant skills, evolving your mindset, and maintaining balance, you can navigate the shifting landscape of finance with confidence and clarity.

Epilogue: Your New Money Story

Six months ago, Sarah reached out to me with a message that encapsulated the change she had worked toward: "It's different now," she said, her voice steady. "Money doesn't control me anymore, we work together."

Her words were a reflection of the deep shift she had made in her relationship with money. The change, she admitted, wasn't instant, it was gradual, even imperceptible at first. But over time, she noticed how her thoughts, her feelings, and her actions around money had transformed. No longer a source of stress or confusion, money became a tool in her hands, supporting her goals rather than dictating her life.

This shift is what happens when we rewrite our financial narrative. As you've learned, financial well-being is not a destination but a journey, one that's as unique as you are. Your path won't follow a straight line, and that's perfectly fine. What matters is that you remain true to your values and goals, writing your own story with intention.

The Evolution of Your Money Story

Everyone's money story is different. For some, the focus might be on daily financial habits, while others may prioritize understanding the deeper decision-making frameworks. Some of you will find that preparation for future changes is key, while others will begin by reshaping your mindset.

Consider David, a former client who struggled with inherited beliefs around money. His parents had always viewed wealth as something to be earned through hardship and sacrifice, and for years, David carried this belief. But through conscious effort and the tools he learned here, David gradually rewrote that narrative. He honored his family's legacy but created space for his own financial identity, one that embraced growth, abundance, and possibility.

Today, David teaches his children that financial growth comes not only from hard work but from understanding the dynamics of money, the psychological side, the decision-making process, and, importantly, the values that should guide those decisions. Through his own journey, he's created a new financial story that blends both success and struggle, offering his family the lessons they need to thrive in the future.

Your Next Chapter Begins Now

The tools and frameworks you've encountered here aren't just strategies to implement; they are writing instruments to help you craft the next chapter of your financial life. As you reflect on the changes, you've already begun to make, consider this: every decision, every moment of awareness, and every shift in behavior adds a new layer to your evolving story. And just like a well-written narrative, your financial story, grows more nuanced and meaningful with each choice.

You are the author of your money story. The chapters that came before, whether filled with struggle or success, have contributed to who you are today. But they don't define your future. It is within your power to continue shaping the plot. You can choose the direction, the tone, and the outcomes that follow.

Key Lessons for Your Story

As you move forward, remember these key lessons:

- Your past doesn't define you. The stories you've been told about money and the ones you've told yourself are important, but they are not your future.

- Small, consistent actions lead to meaningful change. Financial mastery isn't about grand gestures but the daily choices that compound over time.
- Financial decisions reflect your deeper values. Each choice you make is an opportunity to reflect what truly matters to you, your goals, your dreams, and your priorities.
- Adaptation and growth go hand in hand. Life is constantly evolving, and your financial story should evolve with it. Flexibility and learning are essential components of a well-lived financial life.